Table of Contents

The Best 5 fast Dressing recipes ....

    Balsamic Vinaigrette ....

    Italian Salad dressing 7

    Quick Ranch 8

    Eggless Caesar 9

    Creamy Blue Cheese Dressing..10

More Dressings 11

    Strawberry Vinaigrette 12

    Blueberry Vinaigrette..13

    Italian dressing 14

    Creamy coconut dressing...15

    Orange Dressing...16

    Best Dijon Dressing 17

    Pink Vinaigrette..18

    Warm Nut dressing 19

    Warm Bacon Dressing..20

    Hollywood Italian dressing...21

    Poppy Seed Dressing..22

    Russian Dressing 23

    Your House seasoning dressing 24

    Chunky Blue Cheese Dressing..25

    French Dressing 26

Homemade Dressings 27

    Honey Mustard Dressing 28

    Ginger Dressing..29

    Outback Ranch Dressing 30

Vegan Ranch Dressing..31

Italian Restaurant mock dressing..32

Thousand Island dressing..33

Catalina Dressing 34

Mock Applebee's Oriental dressing 35

Vermont Styled Dressing 36

Spaghetti Factory Mock Dressing 37

Dressing Your Salad: 50 Salad Dressing Recipes That Are Easy to Make and Taste Phenomenal

All rights Reserved. No part of this publication or the information in it may be quoted from or reproduced in any form by means such as printing, scanning, photocopying or otherwise without prior written permission of the copyright holder.

Disclaimer and Terms of Use: Effort has been made to ensure that the information in this book is accurate and complete, however, the author and the publisher do not warrant the accuracy of the information, text and graphics contained within the book due to the rapidly changing nature of science, research, known and unknown facts and internet. The Author and the publisher do not hold any responsibility for errors, omissions or contrary interpretation of the subject matter herein. This book is presented solely for motivational and informational purposes only.

The Best 5 fast Dressing recipes

Balsamic Vinaigrette

Ingredients:
- ¾ C EVOO
- ¼ C balsamic vinegar
- Salt and pepper to taste

Directions:

1. Add ingredients to a mason jar and seal tightly.

Italian Salad dressing

Ingredients:
- 1 C neutral oil salad
- ¼ C white wine vinegar
- 1 T minced garlic
- 2 T finely chopped shallots
- 2 T chopped red bell pepper
- 2 tsp Dijon
- 1 tsp honey
- Salt and pepper to taste
- ¼ tsp dried oregano
- ¼ tsp dried marjoram
- 1 tsp red pepper flakes

Directions:

1. Add everything together in a jar with tight fitting lid. Shake VERY well to make sure this is thick.

Quick Ranch

Ingredients:
- 2 T cultured buttermilk
- 1 T mayo
- Salt and pepper to taste
- ½ tsp rice vinegar
- ¼ tsp minced garlic
- 3 tsp chopped fresh chives

Directions:

1. Whisk together mayonnaise and buttermilk, season to taste with salt and pepper.
2. Combine additional ingredients and add to mayo milk. Keep cool and good up to 3 days.

Eggless Caesar

Ingredients:
- 5 anchovy filets
- 3 T minced garlic
- 1 tsp salt and pepper to taste
- ¼ C lemon juice
- 2 T red wine vinegar
- 1 T Dijon mustard
- ½ C EVOO
- ½ C parmesan, grated

Directions:
1. Bash the anchovies.
2. Add garlic, pepper and anchovies and set aside
3. Whisk lemon juice, vinegar, and mustard. Whisk in oil. Stir in parmesan.
4. Add everything into blender and puree.
5. Keep cold in refrigerator and good for up to one week.

Creamy Blue Cheese Dressing

Ingredients:
- 1 C crumbled blue cheese
- ¼ C sour cream
- /4 C buttermilk
- 2 T mayo
- 2 T lemon juice
- Salt and pepper to taste

Directions:

1. In a bowl mask the cheese and sour cream. It will come out pasty.
2. Stir in remaining ingredients, and season to taste with salt and pepper

More Dressings

Strawberry Vinaigrette

Ingredients:
- 1 C sugar free strawberries preserves
- ¼ C balsamic vinegar
- ¼ C Dijon mustard
- ½ tsp ground red pepper flakes
- ½ C EVOO
- ½ C water

Directions:
1. Whisk together everything but the oil until well combined.
2. Gradually add the EVOO and serve immediately. Keep chilled

Blueberry Vinaigrette

Ingredients:
- 1 C fresh blueberries
- ¼ C EVOO
- 2 T orange marmalade
- 2 tsp lemon juice
- 1 tsp Dijon mustard
- ¼ tsp salt

Directions:

1. In a blender combine blueberries (half) with remaining ingredients, and blend until smooth.
2. Drizzle dressing, over salad and add remaining blue berries

Italian dressing

Ingredients:
- ½ C EVOO
- ¼ C white vinegar
- 3 T water
- 1 pack Italian salad dressing mix
- 3 T mayo
- 1 tsp sugar
- ½ tsp Italian seasoning
- 1 tsp fresh parsley chopped
- ¼ tsp salt
- ½ tsp lemon juice

Directions:
1. In a bowl whisk the first four ingredients. Then stir in remaining ingredients
2. Serve immediately can keep cold.

Creamy coconut dressing

Ingredients:
- 1 can cream of coconut
- ¼ C cider vinegar
- 1 package dry Italian dressing

Directions:

1. Add everything in a mixing bowl and mix appropriately.
2. Serve chilled

Orange Dressing

Ingredients:
- ½ C pineapple bites
- 1 can mandarin oranges
- 2 T dried parsley flakes
- 2 T lemon juice
- 2 T honey
- 2 T vegetable oil
- ¼ salt and pepper

Directions:

1. In food blender add everything and puree. Serve and cover

Best Dijon Dressing

Ingredients:
- 1 C vegetable oil
- ½ C cider vinegar
- ¾ tsp salt
- 1 T Dijon mustard
- 1 T grated onion
- 1 T sugar

Directions:
1. In a medium bowl whisk everything.
2. Serve, cover and chill.

Pink Vinaigrette

Ingredients:
- 1 C cut up seeded watermelon
- ½ C frozen raspberries
- 2 T honey
- 1 T white vinegar

Directions:

1. In processor blend watermelon and raspberries until smooth
2. Add remaining ingredients and pulse. Serve and/or store chilled

Warm Nut dressing

Ingredients:
- 2 T peanut oil
- ¼ C chopped walnuts
- 1/3 C honey
- ¼ C maple syrup
- ½ C bottled Italian dressing
- 2 heads romaine lettuce
- 1can sweet pitted cherries

Directions:

1. Drain cherries, chop lettuce and dice walnuts.
2. Sauté the nuts in skillet until browned lightly.
3. Add everything else but the lettuce and simmer for about 6 minutes
4. Add lettuce in a bowl, toss with dressing.
5. Top with cherries

Warm Bacon Dressing

Ingredients:
- 1 lbs. bacon, diced or crumbled
- ½ C apple cider vinegar
- 1 T fresh lemon juice
- ¼ C sugar
- ½ tsp pepper

Directions:

1. In skillet cook bacon, drain grease, crumble bacon.
2. Add ret of ingredients and mix well. Want to serve warm.

Hollywood Italian dressing

Ingredients:
- ¾ C mayo
- 1 T vegetable oil
- ¼ C white vinegar
- 1 T lemon juice
- ¼ C parmesan cheese
- 1 T sugar
- 2 T minced garlic
- ½ tsp Italian dressing
- ½ tsp salt

Directions:

1. Blend everything until smooth.
2. Keep cold until serving.

Poppy Seed Dressing

Ingredients:
- ¾ C mayo
- 1/3 C honey
- 2 T yellow mustard
- 2 T poppy seeds
- 1/8 salt and pepper to taste

Directions:

1. In mixing bowl whisk everything together until well combined.
2. Serve immediately or chilled. Keep covered.

Russian Dressing

Ingredients:
- 2 C mayo
- ¼ C ketchup
- ½ C sweet relish
- ½ tsp garlic powder
- ½ salt and pepper

Directions:

1. In a bowl whisk everything together until well mixed.
2. Serve immediately.

Your House seasoning dressing

Ingredients:
- ¾ C cottage cheese
- ½ C buttermilk
- ¼ C grated parmesan
- ½ tsp Italian seasoning
- ¼ tsp salt and pepper to taste
- 1 T chopped sun dried tomatoes

Directions:

1. Add everything into blender and set to smooth. Add to a small bowl or squeeze bottle and serve.
2. Keep cold.

Chunky Blue Cheese Dressing

Ingredients:
- ¼ C mayo
- 1 tsp vegetable oil
- 1½ tsp white vinegar
- 1/8 tsp sugar
- 1/8 tsp salt and pepper to taste
- 1 package crumbled blue cheese
- ¾ C sour cream

Directions:

1. Add everything but the blue cheese together in a bowl.
2. Whisk until smooth.
3. Add blue cheese stirring well, serve, cover when not in use and chill.

French Dressing

Ingredients:
- 1 can condensed tomato soup
- 1 C vegetable oil
- ¾ C apple cider vinegar
- 1 onion, grated
- ¼ C sugar
- 1 T minced garlic
- 1 T Dijon mustard
- 1 T horseradish
- 1 tsp salt and pepper to taste

Directions:

1. Add everything in a medium to large bowl, mixing well. Or blend.
2. Serve cold, cover for storage and chill

Homemade Dressings

Honey Mustard Dressing

Ingredients:
- ½ C mayo
- ¼ C mustard
- ¼ C honey
- 1 T rice wine vinegar
- Cayenne pepper

Directions:

1. Whisk everything together and keep cold.

Ginger Dressing

Ingredients:
- ½ C minced onion
- ½ C peanut oil
- 1/3 C rice vinegar
- 2 T water
- 2 T minced ginger
- 2 T minced celery
- 2 T ketchup
- 4 tsp soy sauce
- 2 tsp sugar
- 2 tsp lemon juice
- ½ tsp minced garlic
- ½ tsp salt and pepper

Directions:
1. Add everything together in a blender.
2. Blend on high for 30 seconds or so.

Outback Ranch Dressing

Ingredients:
- 1 T hidden valley ranch dressing mix
- 1 C mayo
- ½ C buttermilk
- ¼ tsp black pepper
- 1/8 tsp paprika
- 1/8 tsp minced garlic

Directions:

1. Mix everything in a medium size bowl
2. Chill for about 30 minutes before serving.
3. You can add cayenne pepper instead of paprika for added kick

Vegan Ranch Dressing

Ingredients:
- 1 C vegan mayonnaise
- ½ tsp garlic powder
- ½ tsp onion powder
- Salt and pepper to taste
- 2 tsp parsley, chopped
- ½ C soy milk

Directions:

1. Whisk everything together and let chill before adding to any salad.

Italian Restaurant mock dressing

Ingredients:
- ½ C mayo
- 1/3 C white vinegar
- 1 tsp vegetable oil
- 2 T shredded parmesan cheese
- 2 T Romano cheese
- ¼ tsp garlic salt
- ½ tsp Italian seasoning
- 1 T lemon juice

Directions:

1. Mix all ingredients together in blender.
2. Add sugar to taste

Thousand Island dressing

Ingredients:
- ½ C mayo
- 2 T ketchup
- 1 T white vinegar
- 2 tsp sugar
- 2 tsp sweet pickle relish
- 1 tsp minced onion
- Salt and pepper to taste

Directions:

1. Add everything in a small bowl, stirring well.
2. Add dressing to a covered container, and keep cold for several hours. Wait for sugar to dissolve.

Catalina Dressing

Ingredients:
- 1 C sugar
- 2 tsp salt and pepper to taste
- 1 tsp paprika
- ½ tsp ground chili powder
- ½ tsp celery seed
- Minced onion to taste
- ½ C apple cider vinegar
- 2/3 C ketchup
- 1 C vegetable oil

Directions:

1. Add all of above mentioned ingredients and add everything to a blender and mix well.
2. Move to air tight Mason jar or container and shake before using.

Mock Applebee's Oriental dressing

Ingredients:
- 3 T honey
- 1 ½ T rice wine vinegar
- ¼ C mayo
- 1 tsp Dijon mustard
- 1/8 sesame oil

Directions:

1. Blend everything together and store chilled.

Vermont Styled Dressing

Ingredients:
- ½ C olive oil
- ¼ C cider vinegar
- ½ C ketchup
- 1/3 C diced onion
- ½ C maple syrup
- Salt and pepper to taste
- 1 tsp minced garlic
- 1 tsp paprika

Directions:

1. Add everything into a blender and set on high speed for one minute
2. Serve right away or store in refrigerator.

Spaghetti Factory Mock Dressing

Ingredients:
- ¾ C oil
- 1 C mayo
- ¾ C buttermilk
- 2 T grated Romano cheese
- 2 T dried basil
- ½ salt and pepper to taste
- 1 T minced garlic
- ¼ tsp paprika

Directions:
1. Whisk together first two ingredients.
2. Add remaining ingredients and mix well.
3. Let sit overnight in refrigerator. Serve cold (Great chicken marinade as well)

Printed in Great Britain
by Amazon